Your Weekly Journal of

Positive Wellness
and Affirmations

Your Weekly Journal of
Positive Wellness
and Affirmations

Dr. Lisa Blanchfield
Licensed Mental Health Counselor

YOUR WEEKLY JOURNAL OF POSITIVE WELLNESS AND AFFIRMATIONS

iUniverse books may be ordered through booksellers or by contacting:

iUniverse
1663 Liberty Drive
Bloomington, IN 47403
www.iuniverse.com
1-800-Authors (1-800-288-4677)

Because of the dynamic nature of the Internet, any web addresses or links contained in this book may have changed since publication and may no longer be valid. The views expressed in this work are solely those of the author and do not necessarily reflect the views of the publisher, and the publisher hereby disclaims any responsibility for them.

Any people depicted in stock imagery provided by Thinkstock are models, and such images are being used for illustrative purposes only. Certain stock imagery © Thinkstock.

ISBN: 978-1-5320-0184-0 (sc)
ISBN: 978-1-5320-0185-7 (e)

Library of Congress Control Number: 2016911277

Print information available on the last page.

iUniverse rev. date: 07/30/2016

Contents

Introduction vii

Week One .... Life Is Our Teacher 1

Week Two .... Life Breaks Your Heart 3

Week Three .... "I thank you for your part in my journey" 5

Week Four .... You have the Strength To Ride the Storm 7

Week Five .... Small Victories 9

Week Six .... Positive Coping Skills 11

Week Seven .... Mindfulness: Live in the moment 13

Week Eight .... Master of Our Recovery 15

Week Nine .... Your Personal Action Plan and Goals 17

Week Ten .... Faith 19

Week Eleven .... Repetitive Behaviors 21

Week Twelve .... Positive Thoughts for the Future 23

In Conclusion 25

About the Author 27

Resources 29

Acknowledgements/Dedication 33

Introduction

As we navigate through the difficult times in our lives, we may find it useful to counter unhealthy thoughts with positive affirmations. Our goal should be to change negative behavior into a positive experience. We can use the technique of "self-reporting" to help us understand, measure and record our thoughts and feelings. Expressing your thoughts in writing can release the powerful emotions that are attached to our important life events. This is also a healing exercise, which can release our painful experiences from our past.

Self-report measures can identify our levels of happiness, satisfaction, and also distress. In order to reduce stress in our daily lives, specific strategies need to be identified to strengthen our coping mechanisms and enhance our peace of mind. If we can be strong enough to focus on our own health and happiness, we can achieve greater results.

One type of therapeutic intervention that is recommended is Narrative Therapy. Narrative therapy is a powerful strategy that is focused on our self-stories. This approach views self-stories as our own interpretation of our life events but examines how we look inward to analyze the story. For example, any life experience can be reflected on in various ways – depending on who is telling the story. The focus in Narrative therapy is to challenge our life stories and change the outcome through self-reflection. Our stories need to be told, and re-told many times depending on the trauma experienced (Brown & Augusta Scott, 2007).

In the next twelve chapters, I ask you to complete each weekly assignment and during the assignment I also recommend that you check in with a report of how you are feeling on that given day. This can be very therapeutic when we are experiencing distress. How many times in one day does someone ask us "how are you feeling today"? We all have unique life stories, which are ongoing and sometimes difficult to describe. Writing our life story can assist with the acknowledgement of what has occurred and also can promote the healing process. In order to overcome our past, we have to face and resolve our previous unpleasant experiences and/or trauma in order to succeed in the future.

Since our stress level, along with our cognitive and mental states, has a great influence over our satisfaction in life - each life lesson is very important to ponder and describe. The approach of self-reporting will be useful with your ongoing search for life satisfaction and a positive behavioral change. There are many types of stress that can influence our daily functioning. For example, alcohol and drug addiction can overwhelm us and our families to the breaking point. Death, separation and divorce causes a huge void in our lives, which we must also deal with. It is very common to face bouts of depression, anxiety and hopelessness due to environmental stressors.

Whatever unpleasant and damaging experiences we have faced in our lives, if we think only of the best possible outcome ~ it will occur. The mistakes of our past also can be addressed when we bring it to our conscious mind and then in written form.

If you choose to complete the Journal with a clinician, expressing your personal thoughts and feelings in writing can be a powerful coping mechanism. The writing brings the thoughts to words in black and white. Whatever traumatic life event you have experienced, or are now experiencing, will become much more real when we can quantify it and share our personal truths with others.

According to Taylor (1983) the Cognitive Adaptation Theory explains how traumatic life events test our meaning and overall mental and physical strength. How we interpret the situation at hand can determine if the outcome is positive or negative. This Journal is one strategy that we can use to gather and strengthen our coping resources and strategies, and ultimately positive outcomes will then occur.

The overall goal of this Positive Wellness and Affirmations Journal is to strengthen your coping skills through writing in order to predict a more positive outcome and solution to any dilemma. When we focus on our individual problems and develop short-term goals, we can move closer toward gaining control of the stressful situation.

As a trauma survivor myself, I have learned that the amount of control you can gain over your own personal life event can determine your success or failure while dealing with distress. Developing a written plan of action, can reinforce our future recovery. When we experience a serious disruption in our daily functioning, we must gain inner strength and develop the positive skills necessary to survive. Our own interpersonal resources can become the change we need to overcome the traumatic event.

For the past ten years as a licensed mental health counselor, I have listened intently to my patients describe their suffering, explore their personal issues and bravely face the traumatic events in their lives. After countless hours of pondering these issues, I have come to realize that we can try to develop the power from within us to conquer our negative thoughts and turn the negative experience into a more acceptable outcome. The development of our own set of positive coping skills (i.e. journaling, physical exercise, meditation, spirituality, etc) can be the start to a healthier response to the issues we face.

After the disaster of September 11th 2001, there was a dire need for Masters Level Mental Health Counselors to volunteer at the Mayor of NYC's Family Assistance Center to counsel families of the victims. I was extremely worried about the stories I would hear at Ground Zero. I was working at Catholic Charities in Ilion, NY in 2001 and I vividly remember what an amazing colleague, Ann Cross, told me as I prepared for my departure to New York City to lend my counseling skills. My friend Ann told me "Just remember that we have to tell our life story at least 20 times to begin the healing process". This was my motivation to travel to Ground Zero to listen to the tragic stories of 9/11. I hope that this writing tool will help you to focus on your life experiences, and begin your journey in telling your story. Understanding the meaning of the powerful impact your past experiences have on your present life will unfold as you share your thoughts and feelings in writing.

The mind- body benefits from journaling can be accomplished either with a helping professional, or you can do this on your own. I have observed numerous clients/patients make incredible progress through journal writing. They learned that making active positive changes in their thinking and behavior can produce a sense of self-awareness - which has led to their own unique personal growth and development.

Working with a trained professional can also reinforce the positive coping skills that you will need to continue with your healing process. Depending on the professional, and their orientation, they can reinforce strategies to continue your success in this process. I hope that you will continue to use this powerful writing tool to embrace your daily struggles and allow it to make you a stronger person. Good luck in your journey through the life events which we all face, and may this writing and eventual healing process be part of your ongoing self-awareness in the future.

All the Best,

Dr. Lisa Blanchfield
June 2016

Week One ....Life Is Our Teacher

The stressful experiences we face in life can be our greatest teachers, and we learn difficult lessons through self-awareness of the situation. But how can we develop a method to "un-learn" the negativity that comes with the distress? The <u>goal should be to use the life lesson and then move on to a more positive result.</u>

<u>Exercise:</u> Think about a negative life experiences (such as a health crisis, loss of a loved one, family conflict/break-up, abuse, addiction etc) and reflect on the event. Make a list of your reactions and any symptoms that are or were evident when things were breaking down, getting worse, and you were in need of help. For example, increased anxiety, depression, unhealthy habits etc. Then describe how you this story began, and what the outcome was (your part in the story !)

Week Two..........Life Breaks Your Heart

We have all experienced a heart-breaking moment in our lives. Write about the life event, and provide information on the outcome of that experience. What coping mechanisms did you use to survive the story ?

_____

_____

_____

_____

_____

_____

_____

_____

_____

Week Three ....“I thank you for your part in my journey”....... (Author Unknown)

There are people in our lives who have carried us through our most difficult challenges. Write down the names of those people who helped you cope with the stressful event, and try to specify how they were helpful. As my brother Peter told me, "we all need at least one person in our foxhole", who is that person (s) in your life story?

_____

_____

_____

_____

_____

_____

_____

Week Four ....You have the Strength To Ride the Storm...... (Kathy Loun Stilley)

We have positive qualities that give us strength during difficult times. Make a list of your greatest strengths and attributes and identify how those characteristics helped you to navigate through the adversity in your life.

_____

_____

_____

_____

_____

_____

_____

_____

Week Five..........Small Victories

From the "Secret Daily Teachings" by Rhonda Byrne, she suggests that we say "thank you" at every turn. Think about the stressful events you have faced and appreciate the moment. Describe the experience and reflect on why you are thankful for this time in your life story. Include any small victories thus far in the experience.

_____

_____

_____

_____

_____

_____

_____

_____

_____

Week Six...........Positive Coping Skills

One important coping skill is to try and manage your negative thoughts regarding the life event. List ways that you have or will try to reduce any feelings of anxiety or depression that have become evident during the stressful period of your life. Sometimes we are afraid to confront the stressors, list any fears you have of that process.

_____

_____

_____

_____

_____

_____

_____

_____

_____

Week Seven.......Mindfulness: Live in the moment

Mindfulness is a coping method to calm down our inner thoughts of negativity and anxiety. We become overwhelmed with what the future will hold. Try to identify all the negative thoughts you have regarding your stressful situation (i.e. I will not recover from this illness, I will not be strong enough, I feel hopeless etc). Analyze which thoughts only pertain to today. Write the thoughts below.

_____

_____

_____

_____

_____

_____

_____

_____

_____

_____

_____

_____

_____

_____

_____

_____

_____

_____

_____

_____

*********Positive Affirmation : You are more than half way there ************

_____

Week Eight.........Master of Our Recovery

As Joel Osteen has stated " Instead of complaining about what's wrong, be grateful for what's right". When we face a stressful situation, commit yourself to success by listing <u>your strengths</u> and the <u>ways you can recover</u> from the stressful event. This is another strategy of staying in control of our thoughts and feelings. Identify also the person, places or things which will help you achieve this goal.

Week Nine .... Your Personal Action Plan and Goals

As we push forward to achieve our inner strength and peaceful response to stressful life events, create a vision of your plan or goal and place a picture of it in this space on this page. We need to take risks in order to grow. Thinking about and visualizing your goals will help to make it happen !

_____

_____

_____

_____

_____

_____

_____

_____

Week Ten..........Faith

Believing in something of a higher power beyond ourselves or the negative events in our life can empower us. Faith offers a defined set of values we have acquired that helps us in our despair. It is difficult to bear great pain and hardship alone. Describe your faith or spirituality, and how it has or can helped you to gain strength and move forward in your life

_____

_____

_____

_____

_____

_____

_____

_____

_____

_____

Week Eleven ......Repetitive Behaviors

According to Albert Einstein, "The definition of insanity is doing the same thing over and over again, but expecting different results".

Identify a habit or behavior that continues to lead you to the same result (i.e. feelings of negativity, anxiety, depression, weight /health issues, addictions)

_____

_____

_____

_____

_____

_____

_____

Now create a List of the <u>Coping Skills and Behaviors</u> you have practiced successfully and imagine how these skills can be utilized as you deal with the situation

_____

_____

_____

_____

_____

_____

_____

_____

_____

_____

_____

Week Twelve......Positive Thoughts for the Future

The greatest weapon against stress is our ability to choose one thought over another (William James).

Now that you have completed your 11 weeks of writing, in the 12th week can you:

Identify how your thinking has changed since you began your writing experience. What have you learned about yourself and your life story?

_____

_____

_____

_____

_____

_____

In Conclusion

~ Mindful Thoughts ~
Finding the Courage

"To uncover your true potential you must first find your own limits ~ and then you have to have the courage to blow past them" (Picabo Street)

Congratulations ~ Your Journal is complete !!! You have achieved the first step in practicing and achieving positive coping skills by writing about your life story and completing your twelve weeks of introspective journaling. In order to dispel negative thinking, we have to replace previous unproductive thoughts with positive affirmations. It is very difficult to navigate through the storms of life without the proper skills to gain success in our journey.

The identification of your limitations is the first step in understanding your greatest strengths. Your personal experience of journal writing will assist with your overall health, happiness and prosperity in the future. After completing this experience, it may be difficult to continue to face the memories we have begun to unfold. During the writing process, those unconscious thoughts and memories we have stored become part of the present. It is not always advisable to bear painful experiences on your own ~ so please consider speaking with a trained professional when and if needed.

Continue to think only of positive and empowering thoughts ~ and only then you will expect and gain different results in your life. It is never too late to make a shift in your daily attitude regarding your past and present life experiences which can influence your future outcome. We can be in control of our worries, health, happiness and prosperity but only when we are fully aware of our negative thoughts. Re-writing our life story is one step in a positive direction,

In order to gain peace and overall happiness in our lives, it is within our power to accomplish this. In reality, no other person can define this for us. Our future is in our hands, and by taking the time to reflect on and write about your life experiences will continue to guide you in a positive direction in the future. Not only should we continue to address our previous breaking points and trauma in our lives, but also strive to gain strength from this for our future peace and happiness. Our life story and experiences have shaped who we are today, and we must be mindful of what we have learned in the past in order to be healed in the present and future.

About the Author

Dr. Lisa Blanchfield is a Licensed Mental Health Counselor with a Private Practive on Staten Island, NY. She was born and raised in Utica, NY and she practiced in upstate New York for many years before relocating to the New York City area. She earned her Bachelor's Degree from St. Lawrence University in Canton, NY a Master's Degree in Counseling Psychology from New Jersey City University in Jersey City, NJ and her Doctorate in Psychology Degree from Cal Southern University in Santa Ana, California. Her career has spanned many years providing psychotherapy for children, adolescents and adults within In-patient facilities in New York State. Dr. Blanchfield holds numerous certifications and has specialized in working with diverse populations. Her clinical experience has been with families in trauma, victims of domestic violence, incarcerated individuals, at risk adolescents, families of 911/ World Trade Center Disaster (Ground Zero), drug and alcohol addicted individuals and children of parental separation and divorce. Her earlier training was at Cornell University where she was a Child and Family Studies Specialist in the Cooperative Extension System for eight years. Her current areas of concentration are Cognitive Behavioral Therapy, Mindfulness -Based Stress Reduction, Narrative and Solution-Focused Brief Therapy and Twelve Step Addictions Recovery and Therapy.

For more information or to contact Dr. Blanchfield:

Dr. Lisa Blanchfield

Licensed Mental Health Counselor

www.Dr-Lisa-Blanchfield.com

email: elgam8@aol.com

2141 Richmond Road

Staten Island, NY 10306

347-882-1719

Resources

AA International Resources www.aa.org

Brown & Augusta-Scott (2007) Narrative Therapy: Making Meaning, Making Lives

Joel Osteen www.joelosteen.com

Kathy Loun Stilley www.havenoflove.com

Meditation Books -Hazelden www.Hazelden .org

Mindfulness Exercises www.living well.org.au

Narcotics Anonymous www.na.org

National Institute on Alcohol Abuse and Alcoholism www.niaaa.nih.org

Picabo Street, Picabo: Nothing to Hide

Rhonda Byrne "Secret Daily Teachings" www.thesecret.tv

Sex and Love Addicts Anonymous www.slaafws.org

Taylor, Shelley E. (1983) "Adjustment to threatening events: a theory of cognitive adaptation" www.psych.ucla.edu

Twelve Steps and Twelve Traditions New York: AA World Services (1976) www.aa.org

William James iep.utm.edu

Your Weekly Journal of Positive Wellness
And Affirmations

Dr. Lisa Blanchfield
Licensed Mental Health Counselor

Acknowledgements/Dedication

This Journal of Positive Wellness and Affirmations is dedicated to my parents, Thomas and Mary Jane Blanchfield. My father, Thomas, was a prolific writer who inspired my clinical writing and also taught me to never give up on my dreams. My mother, Mary Jane, has helped me to define the hardest lessons in my life by understanding the phrase "life breaks your heart". She continues to share with me her strong faith in God and her dedication to a higher power. My parents also supported all of my educational goals which I am very thankful for. To my beautiful and amazing children: ~Jessica, Casem and Tamra ElGamil ~ you love has inspired me to always go on, and I can only hope and pray that you achieve all your goals and dreams throughout your exciting lives. I also thank my children and my siblings for their guidance and the experience of loving me unconditionally. To my past, present and future clients/patients, thank you for allowing me to enter into the private stories of your lives. Your incredible strength to overcome life's obstacles encourages me daily to continue with my vocation and find better understanding of the struggle we call life.